ANASTASIA CHERNYAVSKY

VEVAISWERKDRUCK Nº 42

ISBN: 978-3-945155-42-4

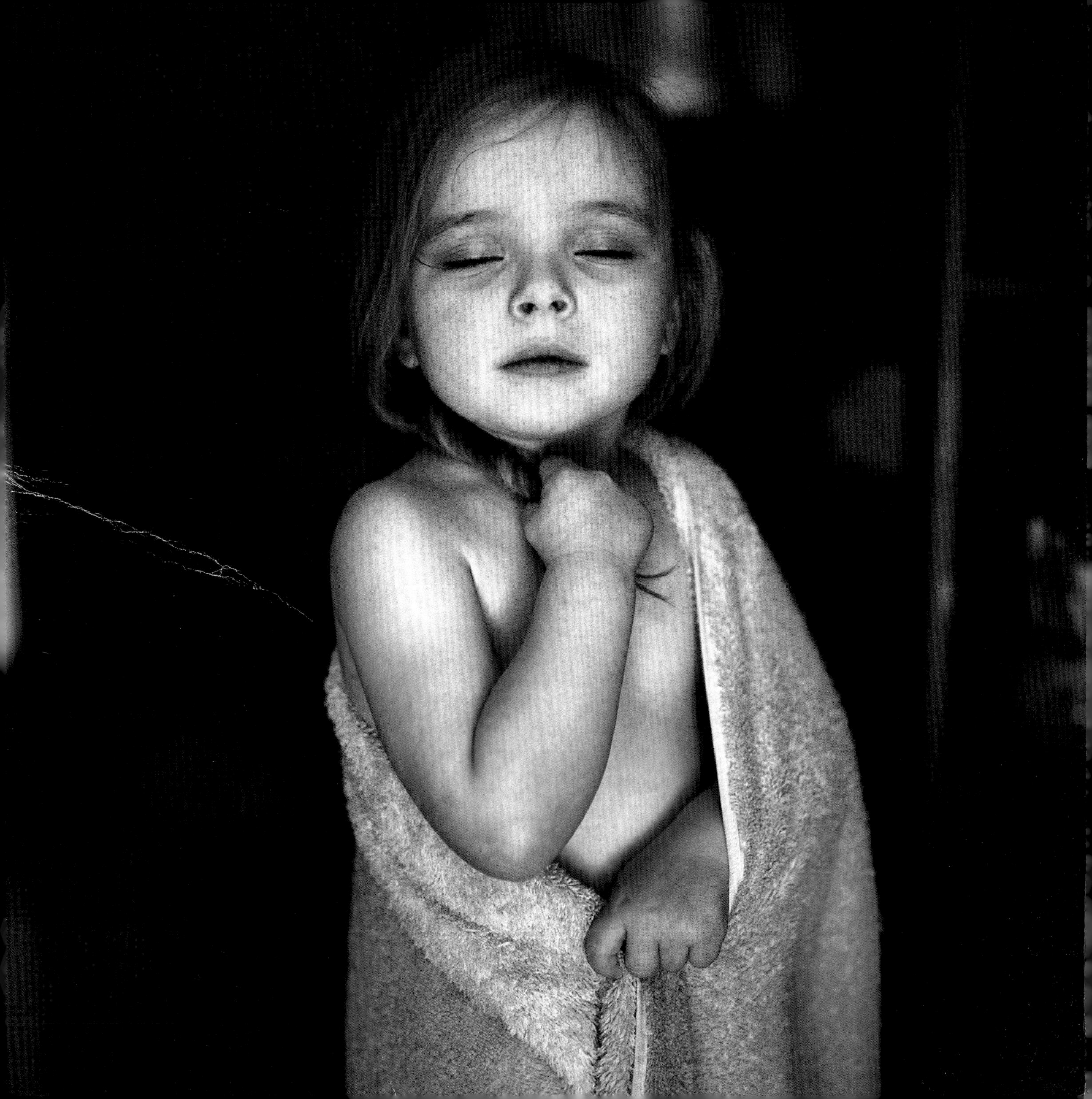

When I was about 7 or 8 my sister and I and a few other children from our neighborhood were bundled up by our grandmothers and herded like a flock of obedient sheep to a church. We were to be christened, whatever that was. I remember almost none of it and retain only the memory of a vast, echoing interior where I was surrounded by the somber, bent backs of praying old women, mysterious in a way that invited no questions.

Some hours later our dad summoned my sister and me for a talk, an event so potent in memory that for me it became "The Talk" for all time. To this day I remember it as vividly as if it had taken place just minutes ago. He crouched in front of us and, taking turns to look each of us in the eye, began: *"So, I hope, you don't believe in God, do you?"*

Imagine the confusion this invoked in my simple child's mind! Seemingly we had already come to know that people were not forever. Thanks to regular planetarium visits, the mystery of human existence against the backdrop of our vast universe had begun to seep into our tender brains. But this man, our father was assuming we knew what "God" was and, over-reaching still further, implicitly admonishing us from becoming devoted to religion.

We were raised in the paradoxical atheist world of the Soviet Empire. Imagine a kaleidoscope of dutiful Easter celebrations with egg-coloring and endless "Christ has risens"s absent any meaning or explanation. In January we often would go caroling. And then we would be carried on shoulders as our parents joined the May and October demonstrations to memorialize the revolution.

So it is no surprise to me that I am unable to pinpoint just when it was that my sense of what or who "God" was coalesced into the certainty that for me the answer to the question was "Conscience". That moment is lost to memory but the sentiment prevails despite many external attempts to channel my mind and soul into more conventional dogmas. This has been my organizing credo for the last 30 years.

Finally no religion appealed to me as a much as a simple joke that evolved out of my sense of what having a conscience means for me. To whit: *"I intend to live forever. So far, all is going exactly as planned!"* And, as it happens. I mean it. I do intend to live forever, and everything truly is going according to plan. For, you see, I am perfectly certain that I will continue to be in my daughters and then in their daughters and then, infinitely so, in the children of their children. This I achieve, atom by atom, by living well, by investing myself, every scrap of poetry and art and caring and disciplined example I can conjur, in my girls. This is everything.

So, this is my art. I appear in many of my images along with the children because they are me, I am them. We repeat each other in in the music of our lives. And when they are alone in the images I am still there. We are a wheel spinning slowly through the light, through the dark, through all of life's doubts and joys.

Anastasia Chernyavsky with Jock Sturges / San Francisco / 2014

Edited by Jock Sturges | Production: Scancolor | Design: Susanne Weigelt | WERKDRUCK is published by Alexander Scholz and Eric Langer.

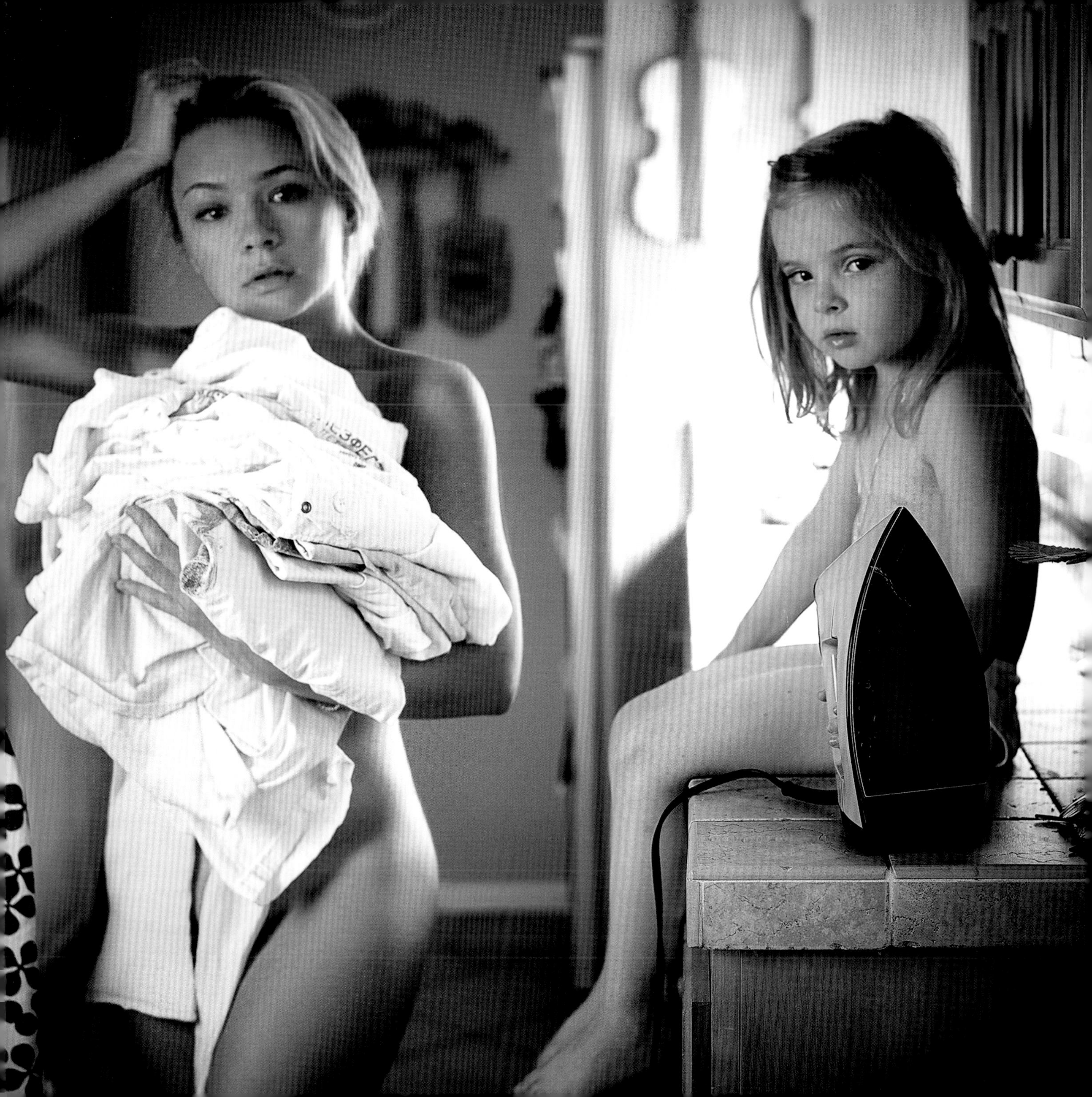

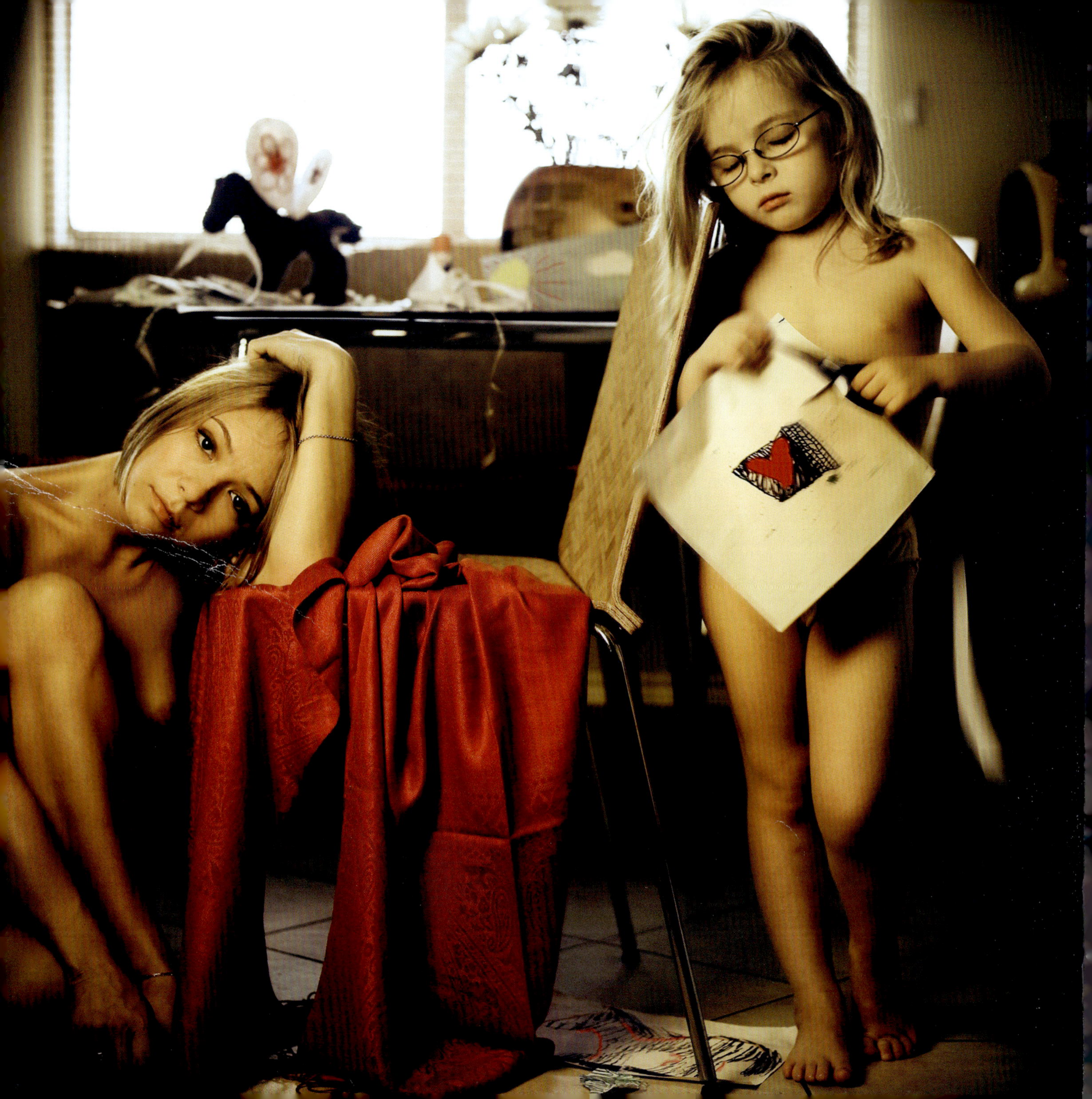

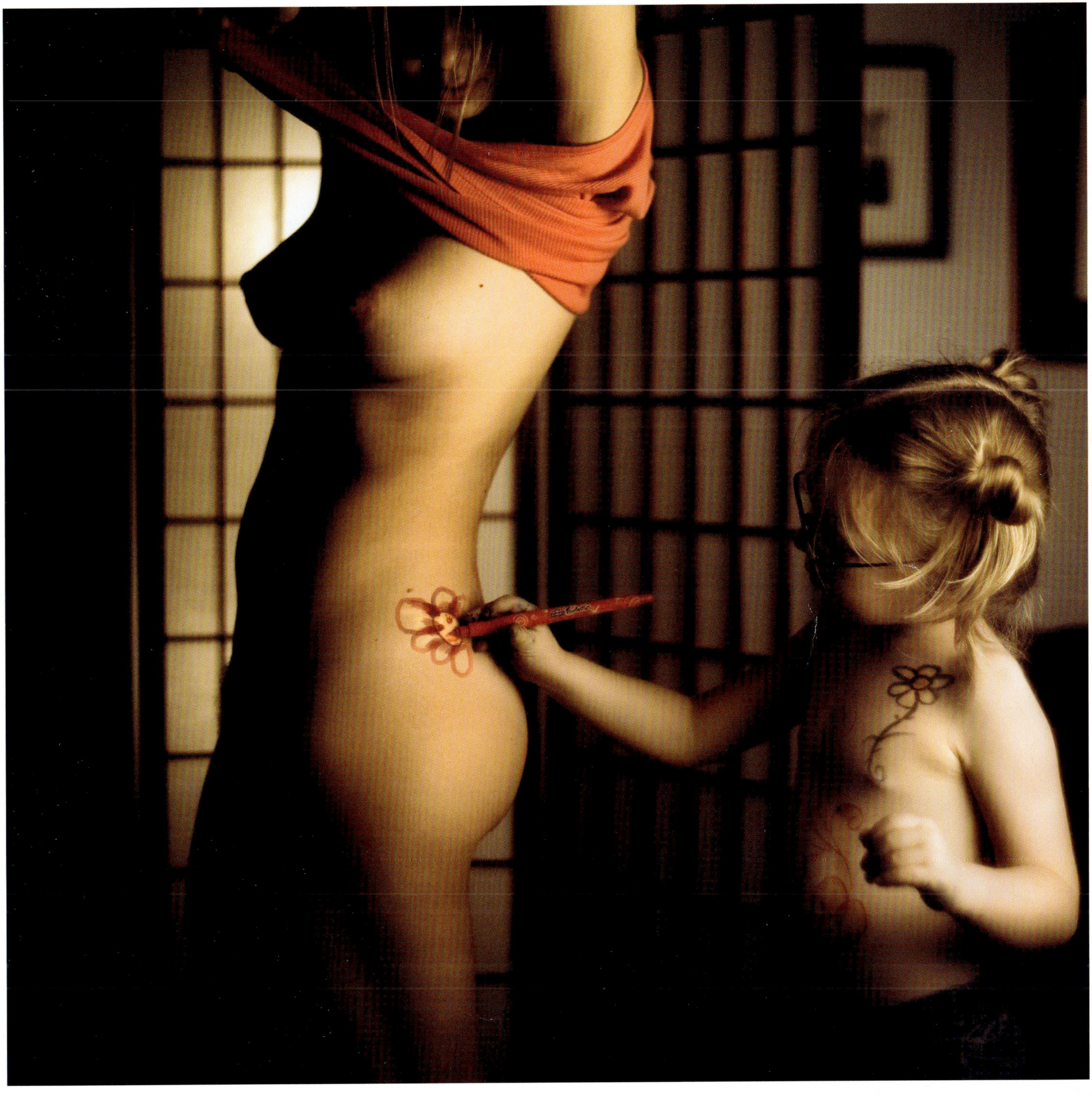

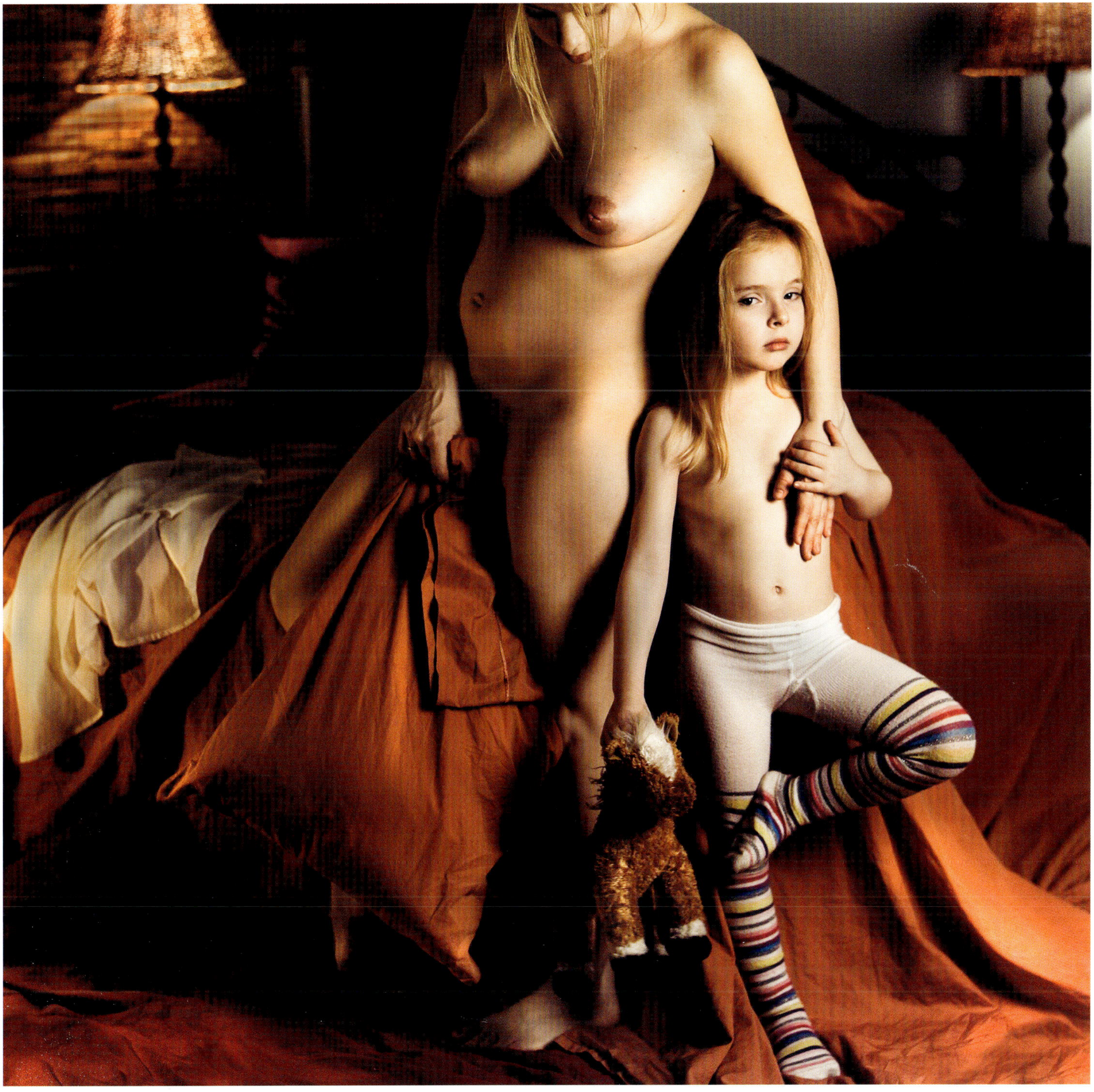

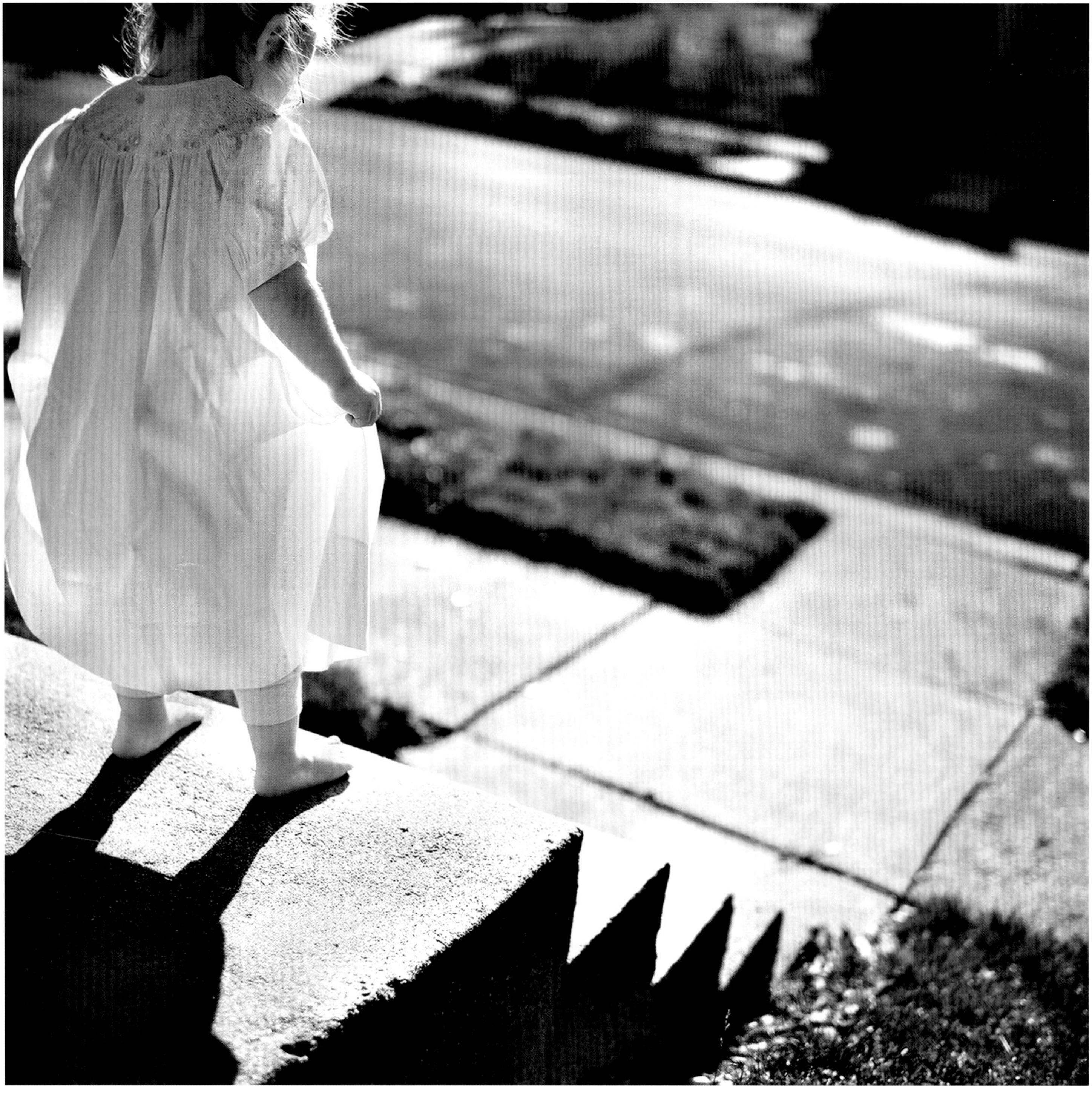

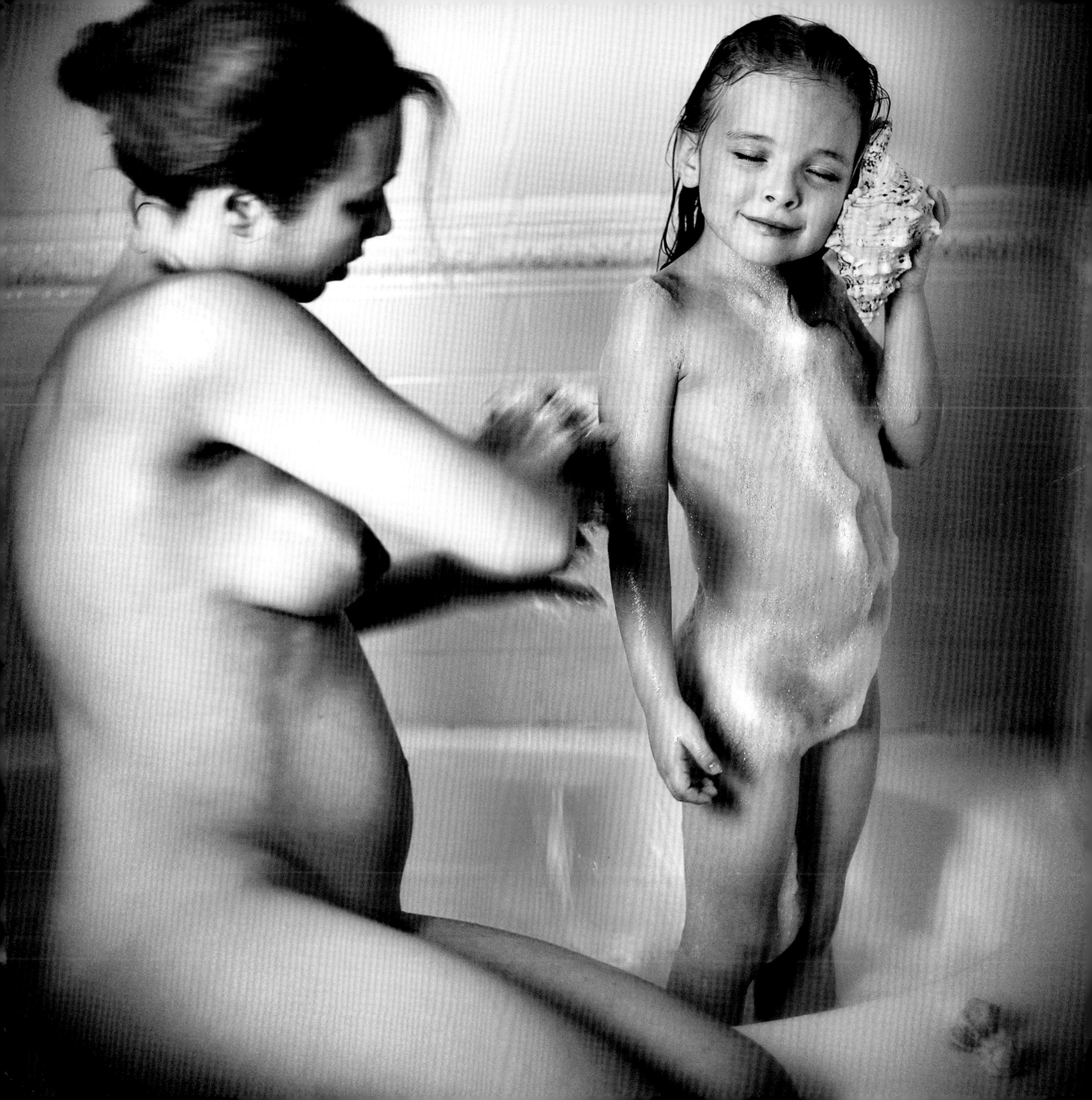

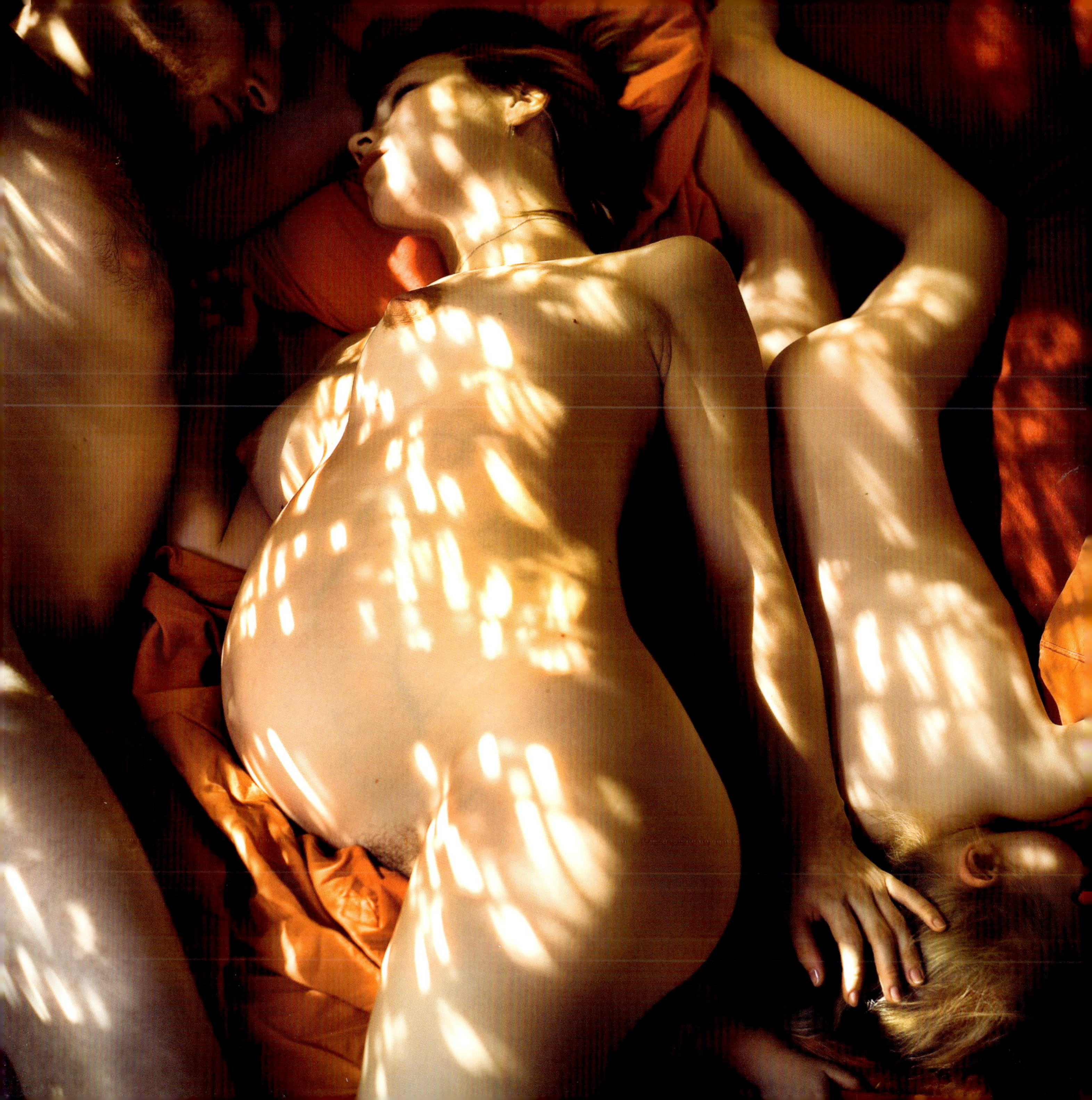

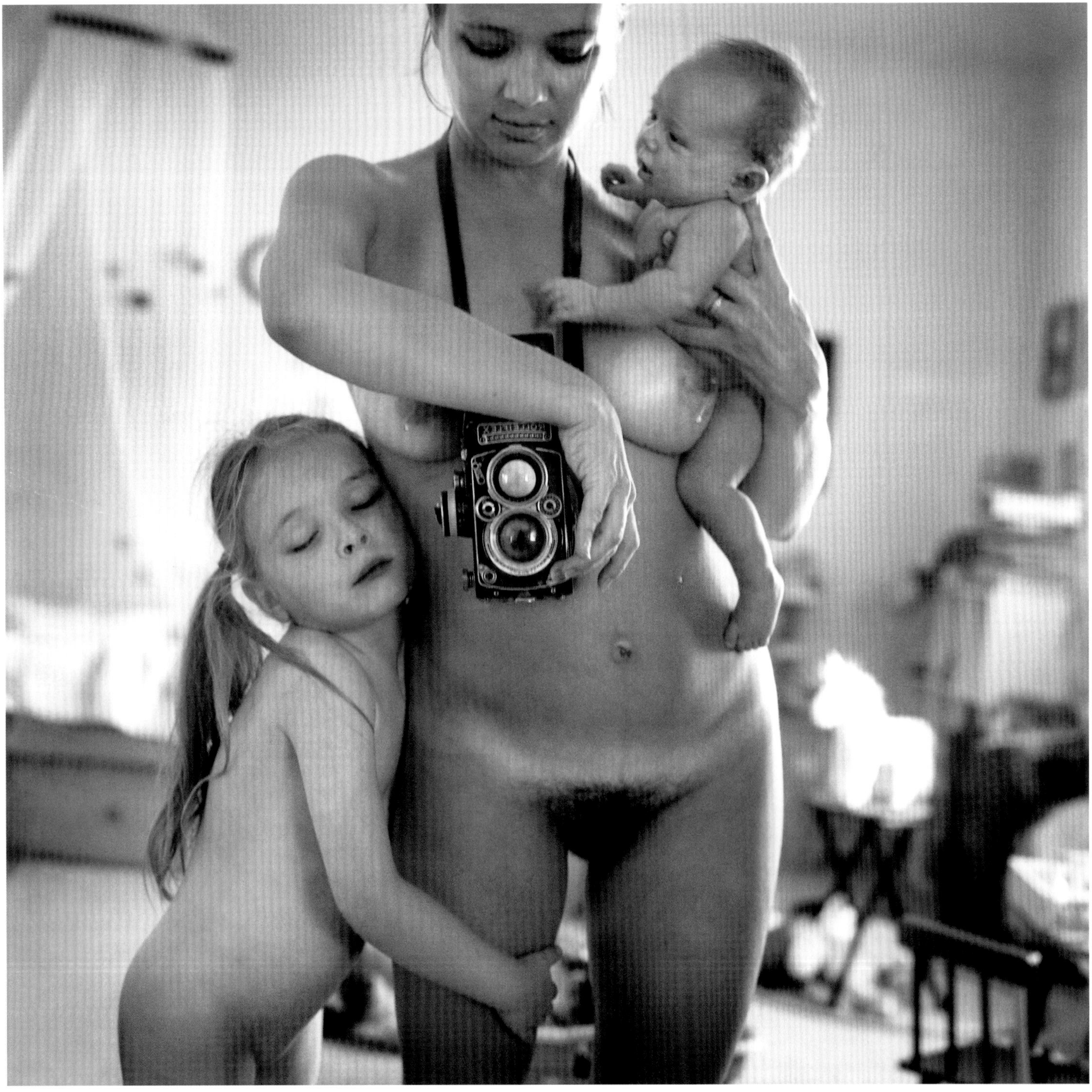

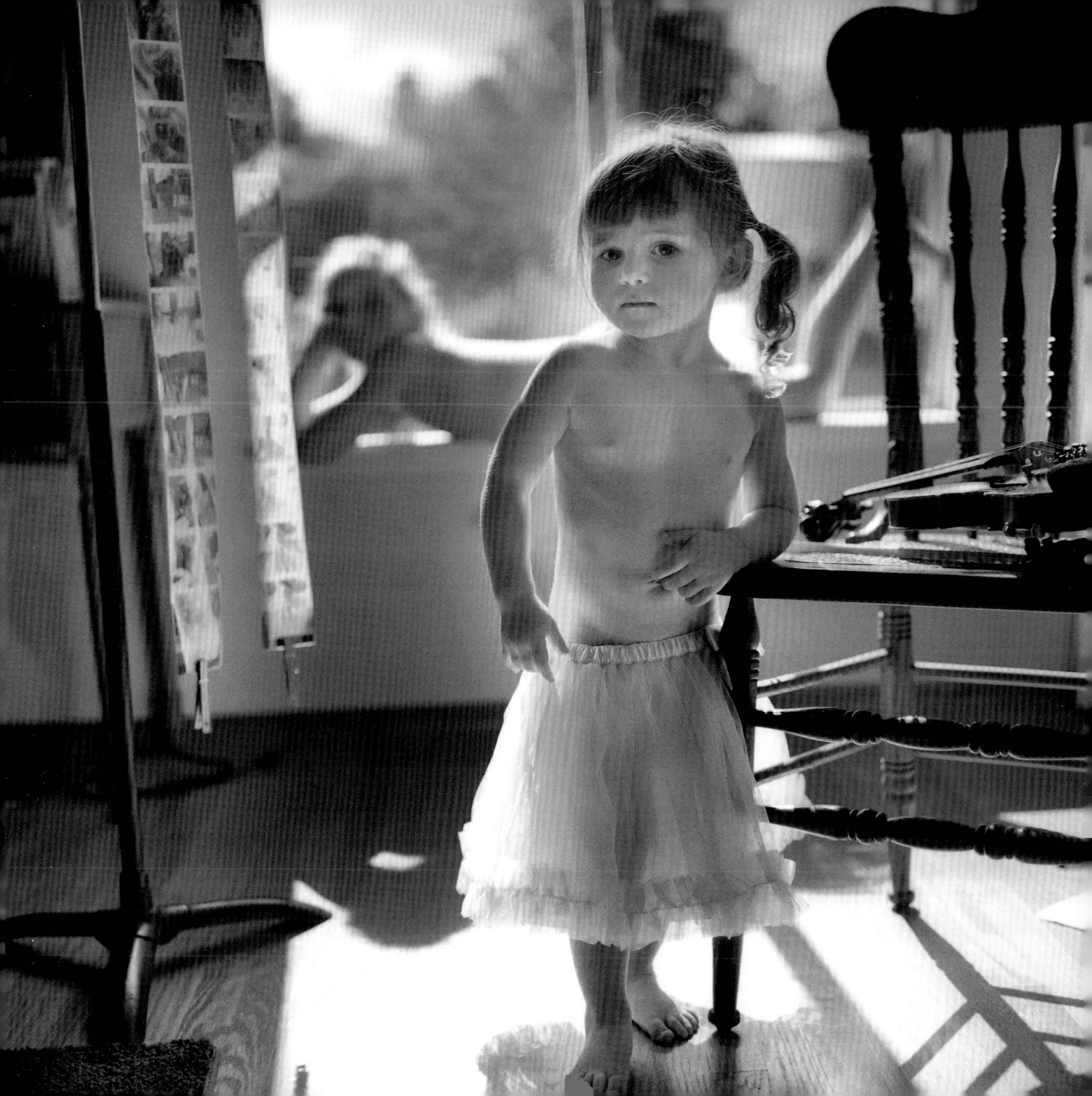

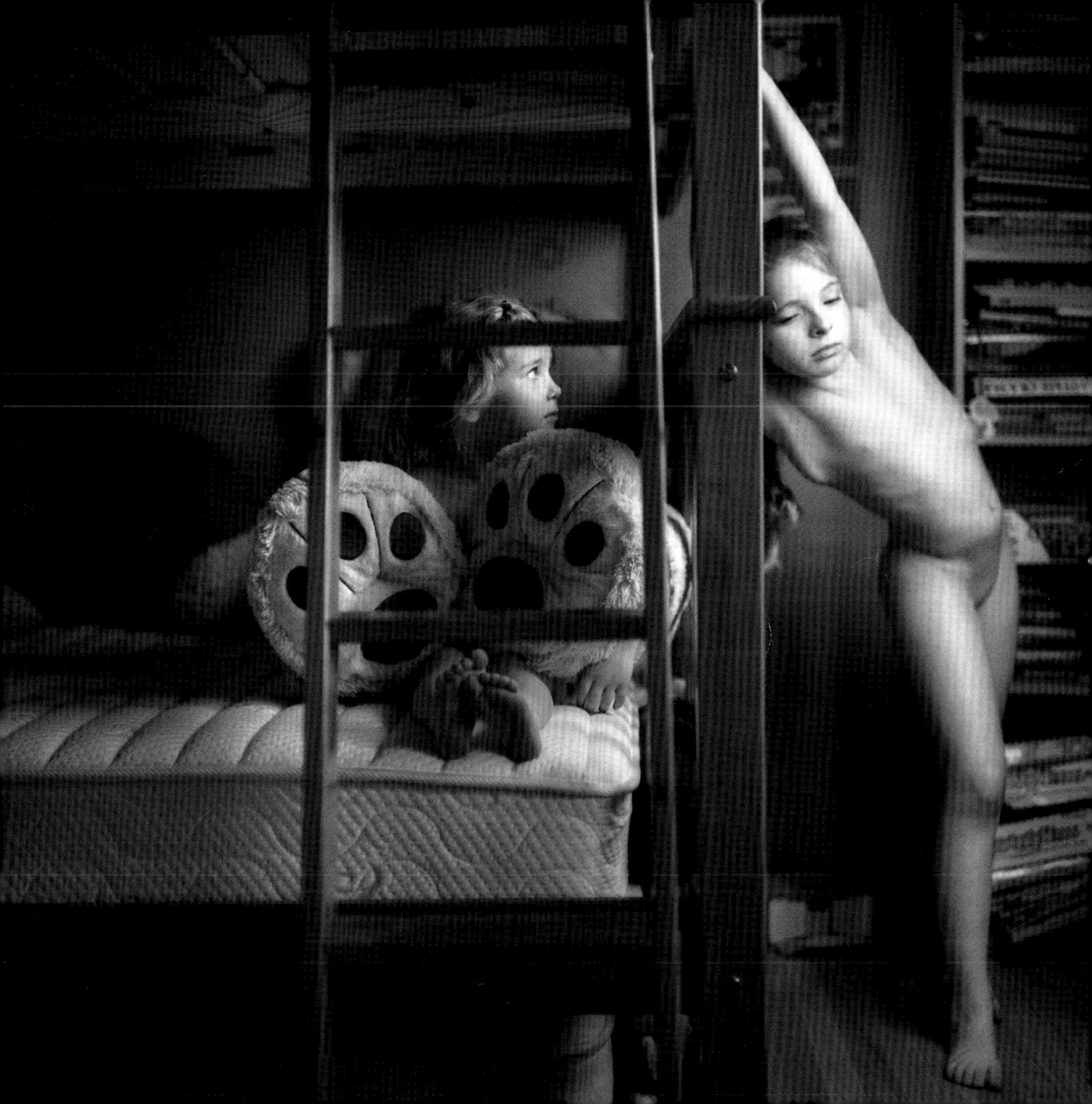

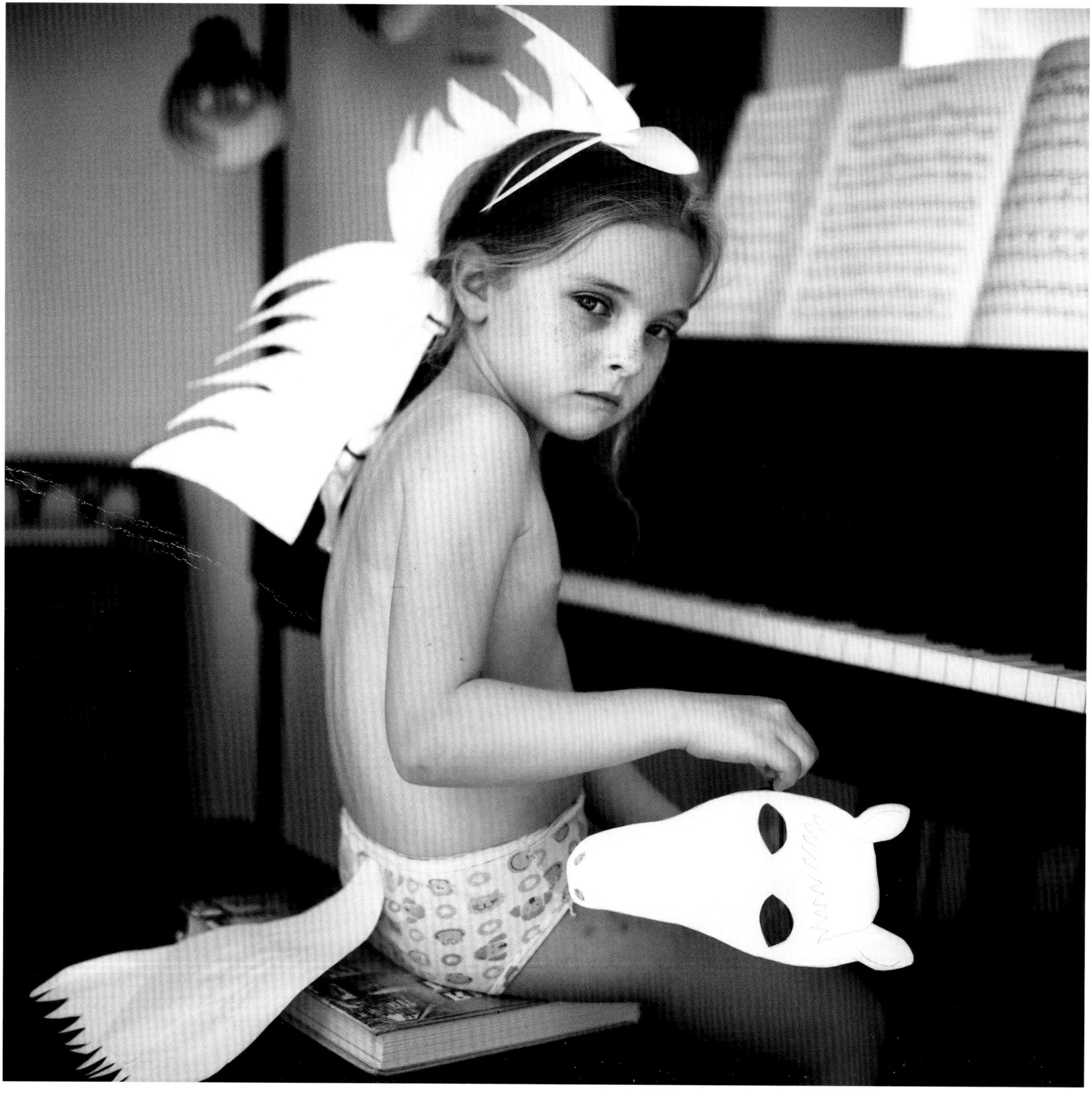

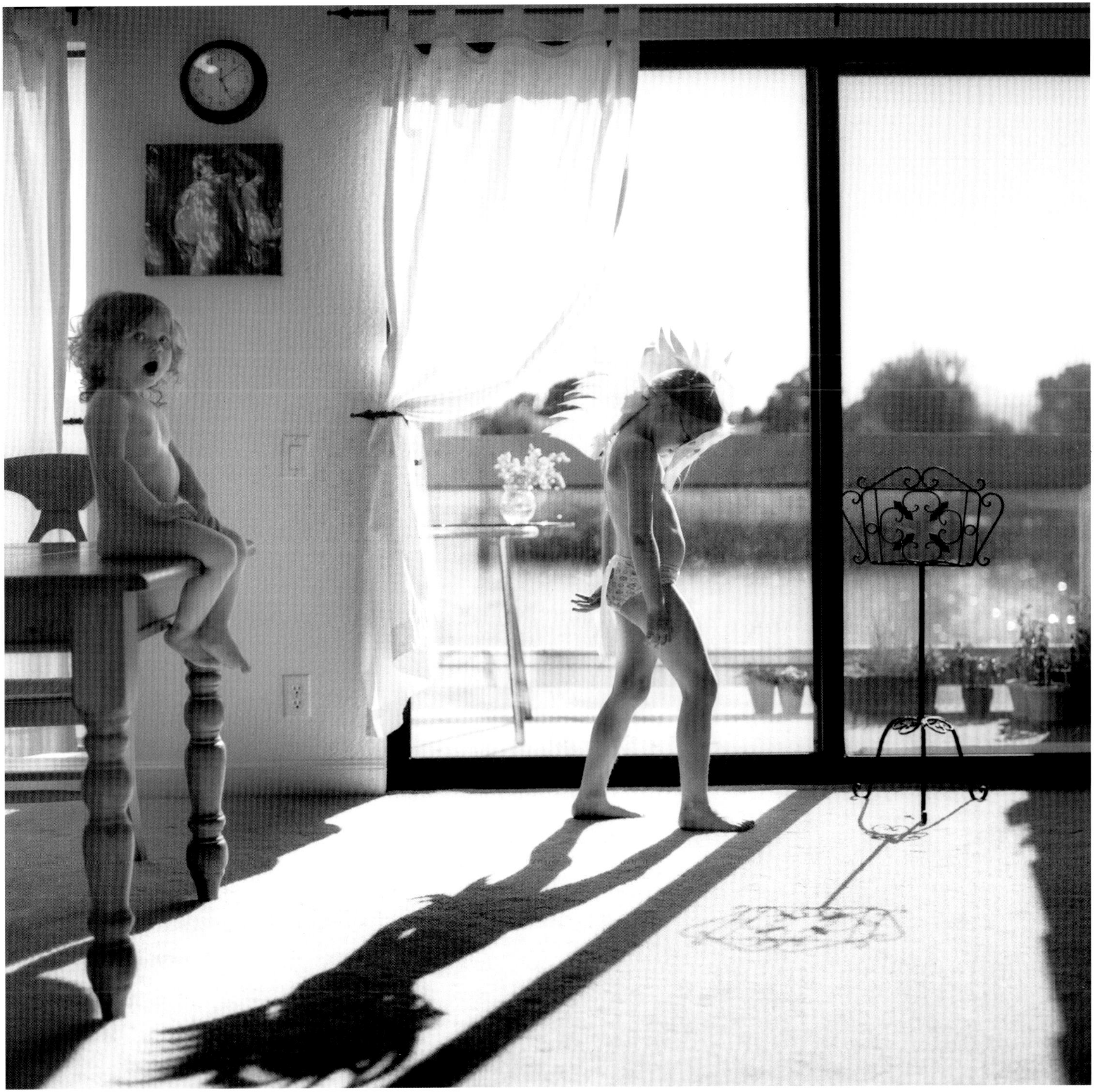

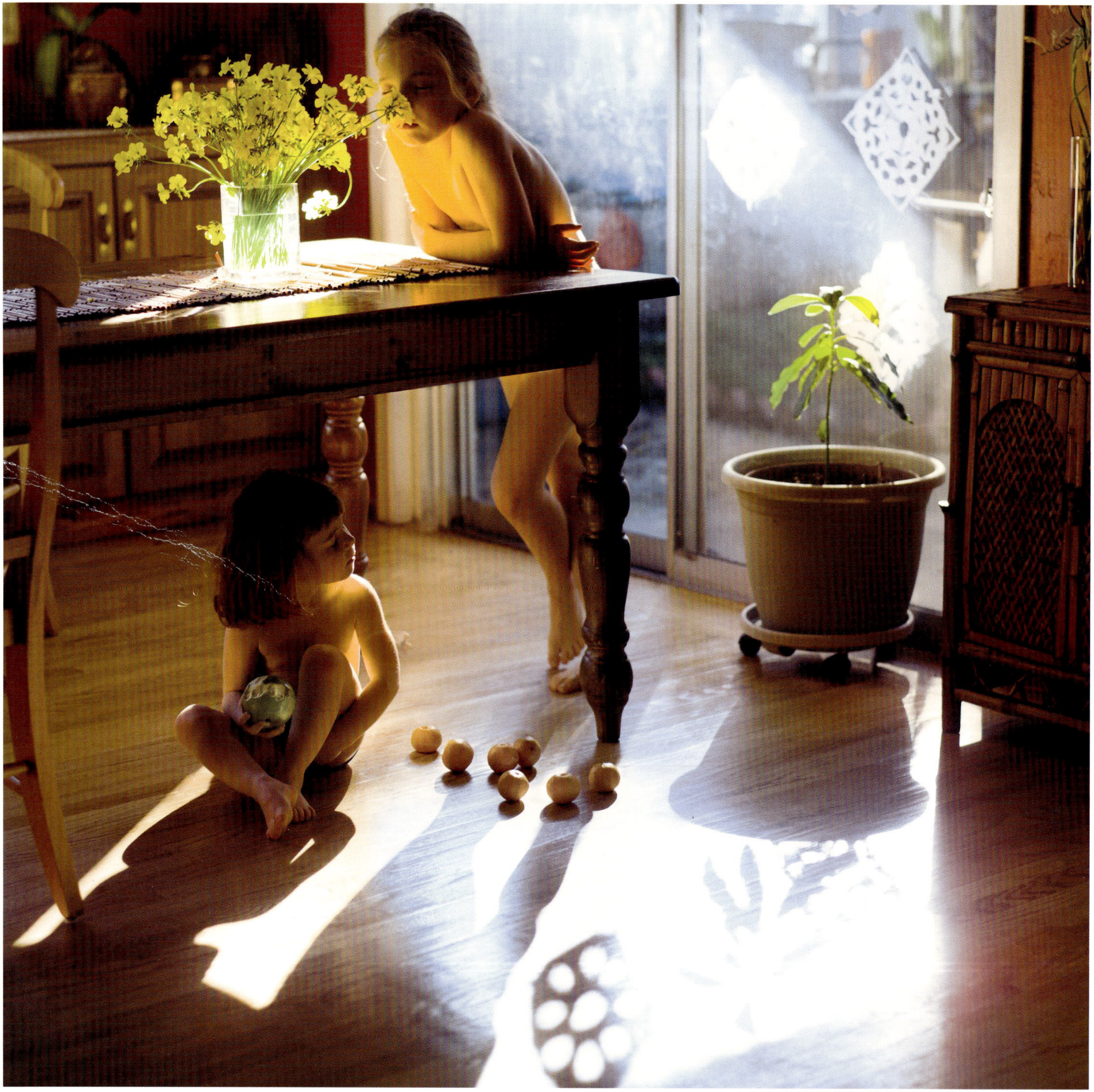

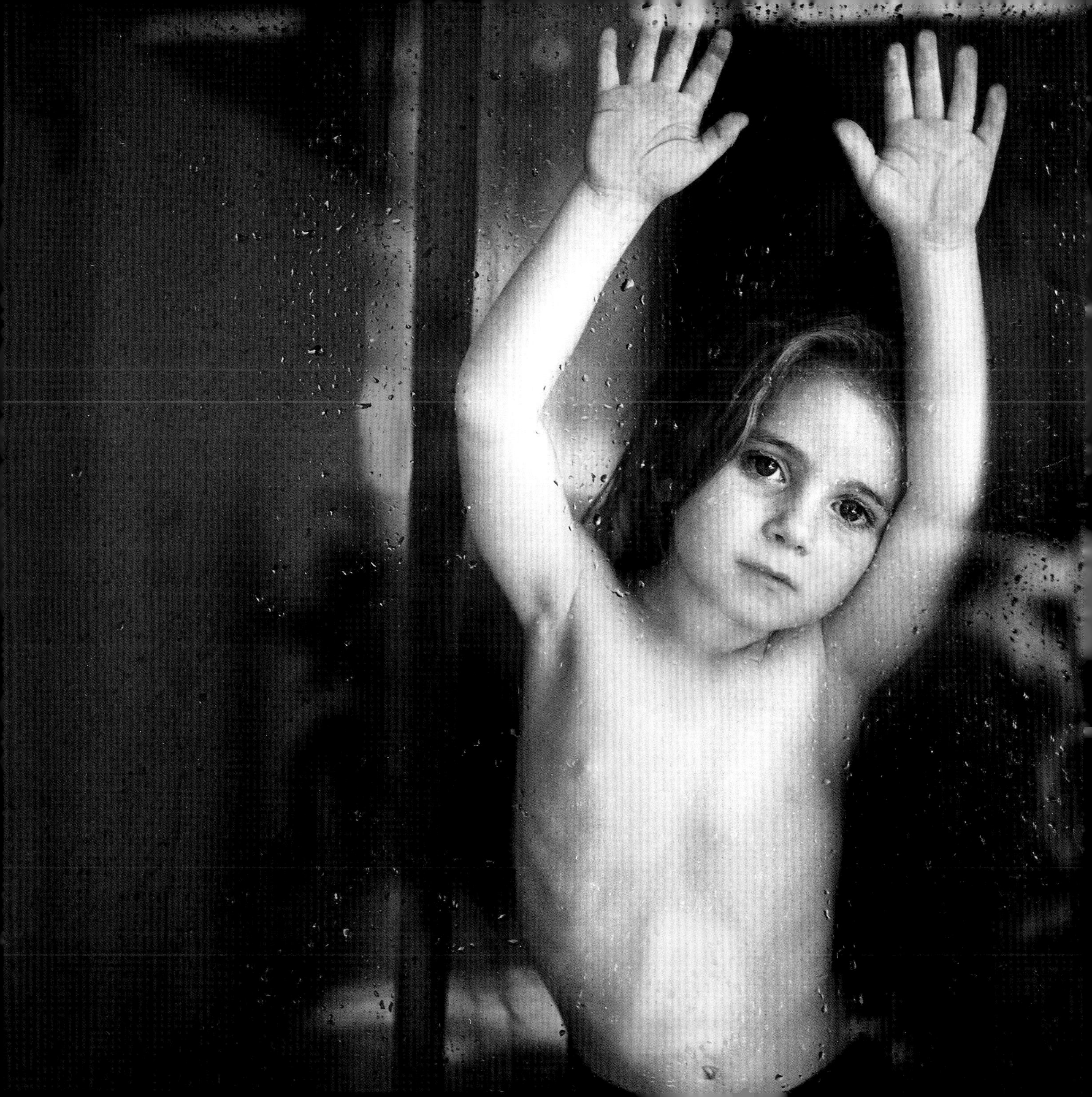

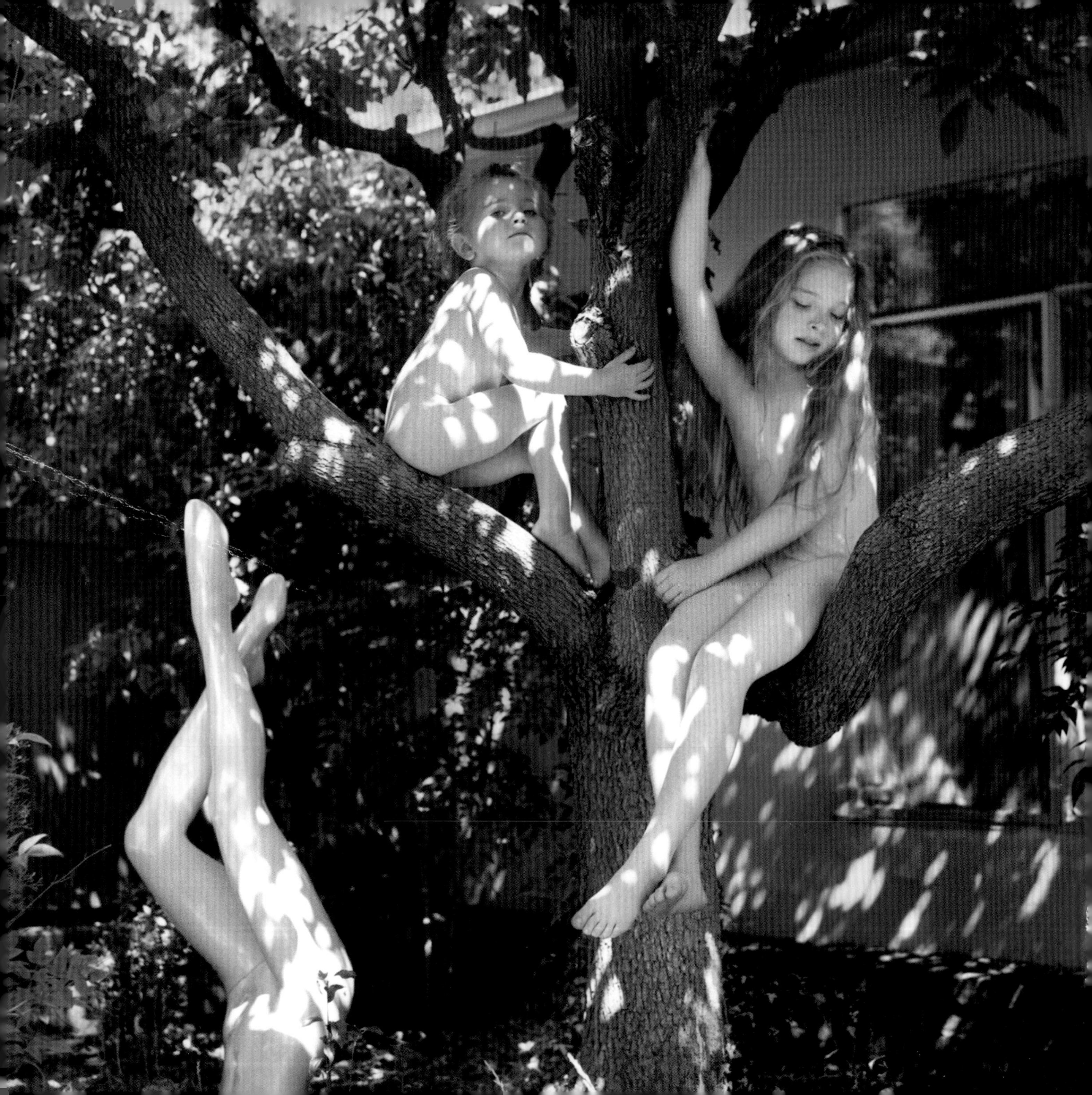

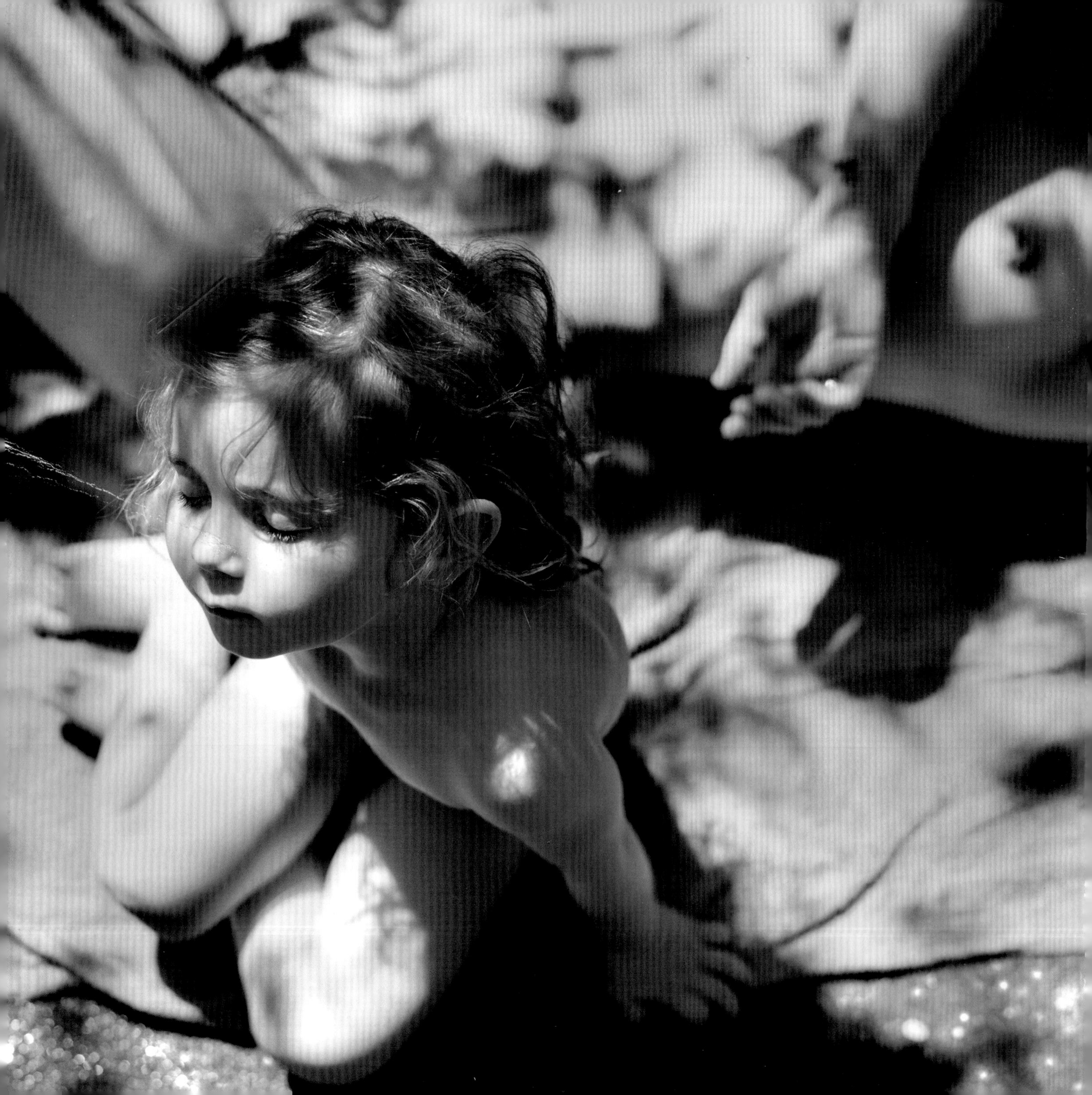

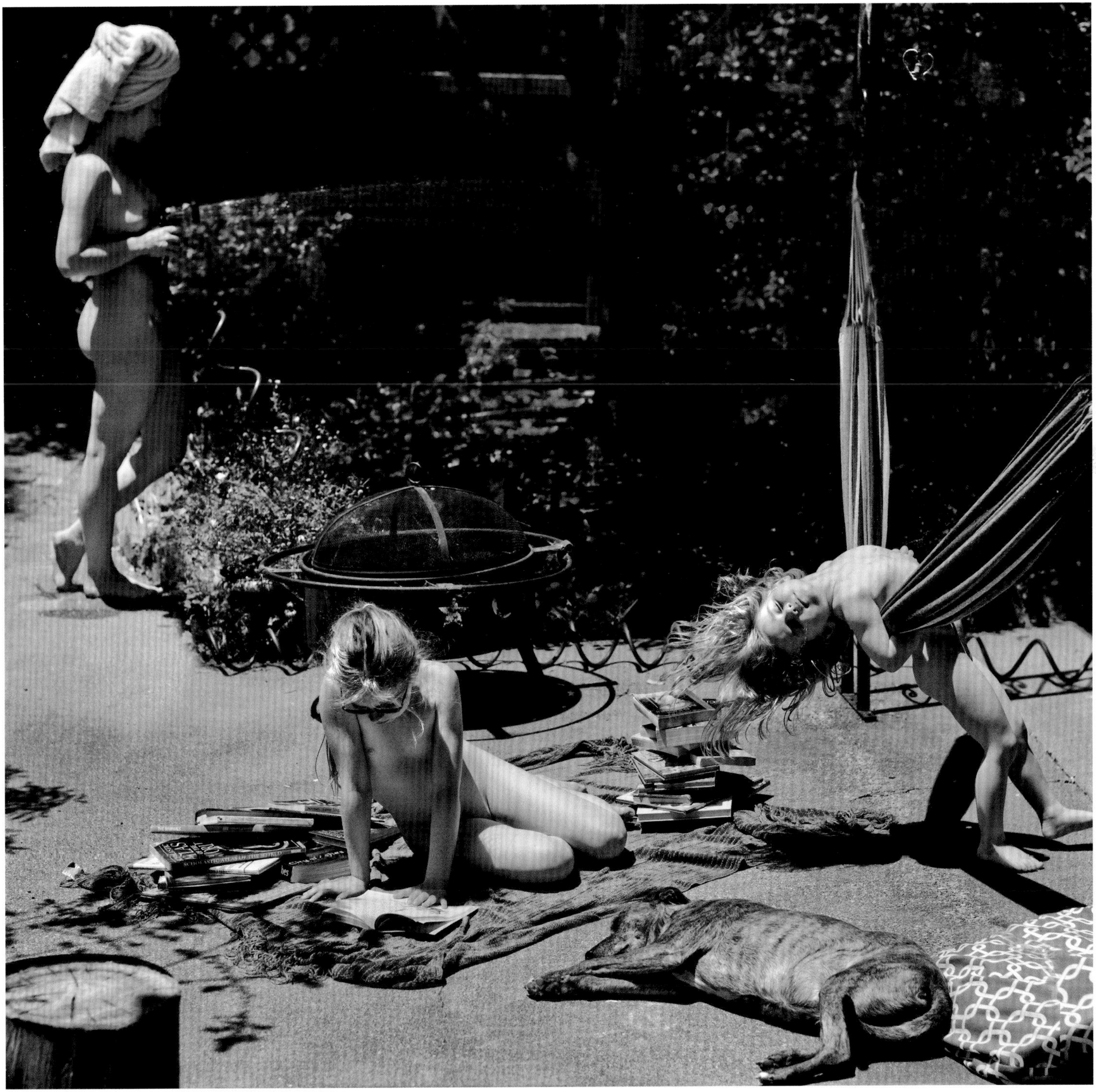

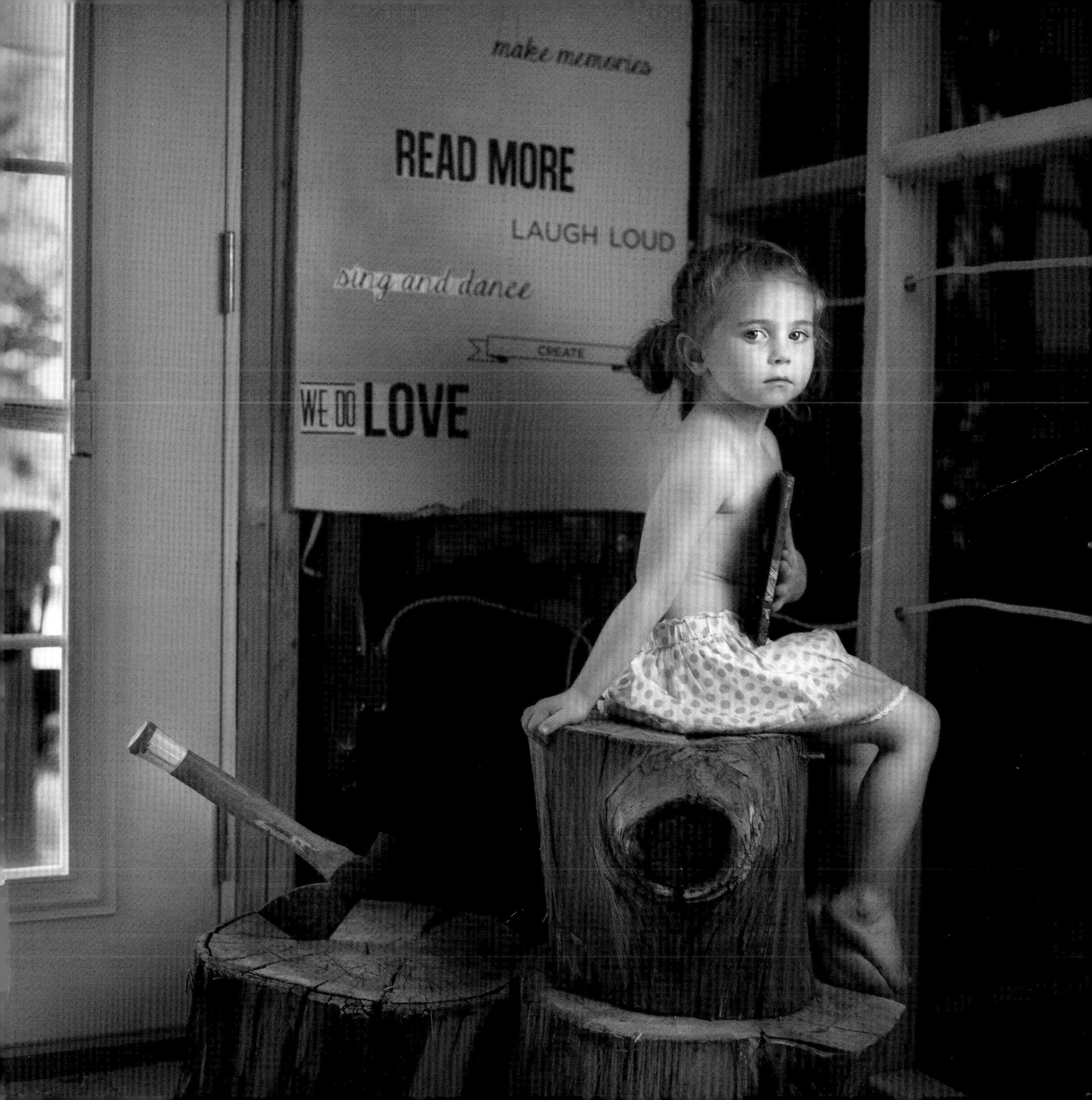
make memories
READ MORE
LAUGH LOUD
sing and dance
CREATE
WE DO LOVE

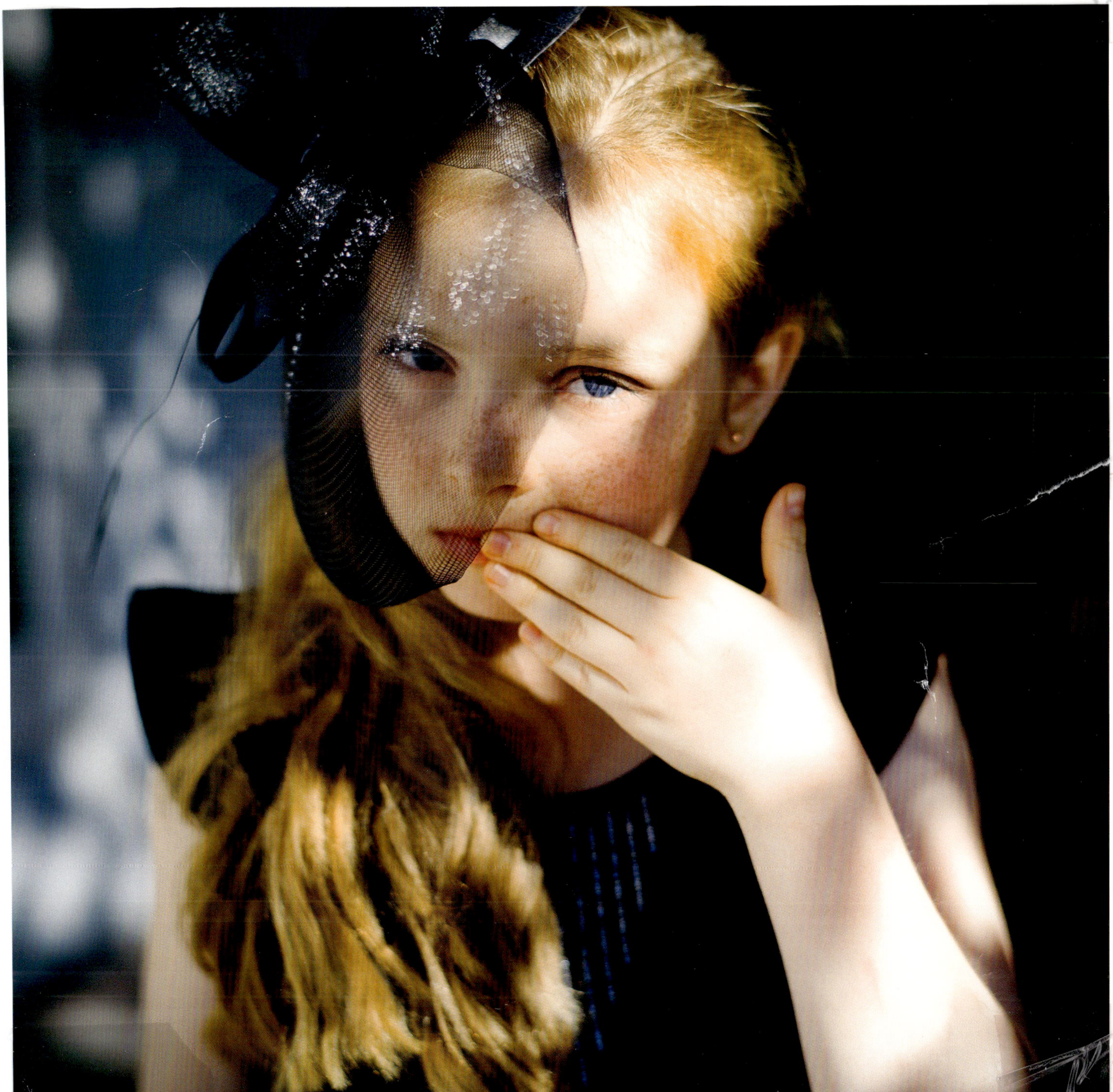